P9-EDR-300

IN THE BEGINNING

The Story of Creation

by

Roger Pilkington

DRAWINGS BY PIET KLAASSE

ST MARTIN'S PRESS · · NEW YORK

Library of Congress Catalog Card Number:
57-12099

From the Revised Standard Version
of the Bible, copyrighted 1946 and 1952

In the Beginning

1: MYSTERY ON THE HILL

One Saturday afternoon when I was a boy I got on my bicycle and started off into the country. I had no particular idea where I was going, but I had decided to explore, so I rode away out of the town and out beyond the railroad yards, and into the valley of a small river which meandered about the countryside.

I rode along a path beside the water, and I had only gone a mile or two before I noticed something rather curious behind some trees about a quarter of a mile from the stream. It was a little hill with steep sides, and it seemed to be a strange bluish gray in color. Deciding to look at it more closely I turned away from the stream and rode down a lane until I found myself at the foot of the little hill.

I leaned my bike against the fence and crawled through. The hill was about twice as high as a house and very steep, and made up of a great pile of grayish powdery stone. I scrambled up to the top on all fours, covering my shoes and trousers with the fine dust as I slipped and struggled up the side. When at last I reached the top I looked down on the other side and saw a big pit full of water. Beyond the water lay some more hills just like the one I was on, and between two of them stood the ruins of a small factory building. It was an old cement quarry long unused.

The whole place seemed dead, a queer kind of relic of days that had passed. Once there had been workmen there, and steam-shovels, and clanking trucks bringing the waste to the heap I was standing on, but now it was deserted. The hinges of a half-rotted door in the ruined building creaked loudly as the wind swung it to and fro. The glass in the skylights was broken in, and here and there the roof itself had collapsed. Work must have stopped here before I was born.

I was just wondering how long it would be before the chimney would fall, when I saw a splash in the flooded pit down below. Yes, there was no doubt about it. A big fish swam there. He had caused the ripples that spread slowly over the surface and died away towards the banks. Once there had been quarrymen digging there, but now there were fishes snapping lazily at the flies.

I turned away and walked around on the flat top of the waste heap. It was all very dull and gray and nothing seemed to grow on it apart from a few scraggly weeds. I was just about to go down

2

the slope to my bicycle and return to the river when I noticed a curious object sticking out of the powdery ground. It was long and thin, and looked exactly like a bone, but when I stooped and picked it up I discovered that it was quite heavy, much too heavy for a bone. It was stone. It was a fossil—a fossil bone, in fact.

I searched the hill very carefully, and by the end of the afternoon I had managed to find about thirty such pieces. Some were whole bones, roundish and flat, about the size of a half-dollar. Others were broken, but a few of them fitted together to make long thin and curved pieces, tapering at one end. I gathered them up, ran down the hill and cycled quickly back home. That evening I packed the bones in newspaper and did them up in a package. Inside the package I wrote a note. 'Dear Sir,' it ran, 'Please tell me what these are and how old, and send them back.' I addressed the package to the Natural History Museum in a nearby city, and next morning I mailed it.

A week later the package returned, and in great excitement I tore it open. Inside was a letter from the assistant curator of the museum. 'Dear Sir,' it said—and as a schoolboy I felt rather grand to be addressed in this way—'The specimens which you sent for identification are ribs, vertebrae, and a paddle bone, all of *Ichthyosaurus,* a large marine reptile. They are separately labeled for your convenience and are returned herewith. The date at which the *Ichthyosaurus* lived would be approxi-

mately a hundred to a hundred and fifty million
years ago. . . .'

As I put the bones away carefully I felt the queer-
est sensation of being somehow in touch with a
world that had existed an incredibly long time ago.
Just as the ruined cement works had been a relic of
workmen who had toiled and steam shovels which
had clanked long before I was born, so these remains of a prehistoric creature told of a very different time far further back, long before the steam
shovels. Where now there was land there had once
been sea, with my *Ichthyosaurus* and countless other
queer creatures darting about in it. As I realized
this my life at home and school, which had seemed
so permanent and unchanging, now appeared like
a single picture taken from a long movie of which
I could not hope to see the beginning.
Next Sunday morning at church school we were
reading the very beginning of the Bible, the first

chapter of Genesis, and it told a story of how God had made the sun and stars and the whole world in only six days. In a queer kind of way this worried me, but when I caught sight of the date 4004 B.C. printed at the top of the page of the old Bible our teacher used I was more worried still. At home I had the bones of my *Ichthyosaurus,* and the man at the museum had declared them to be at least a hundred million years old, yet here was the Bible telling me that the world itself in which my queer creature had lived was created in 4004 B.C. Somebody, I thought, was mistaken. I had been brought up to believe the Bible, and yet it was now obvious that either the Bible or the museum was not telling the truth. I still wanted to think that the Bible was right, but in my own mind I was inclined to think that the museum was the one I should believe. After all, they ought to know.

And if the Bible was wrong about the creation, then surely it might be wrong about other things too.

I didn't like to tell the teacher about my worry. I thought he would be annoyed at my casting doubt upon the Bible. So I just said nothing and learned the Genesis passage word-perfect along with the rest of the class. But on Saturday afternoons I stole back to the quarry. As the months went by I collected quite an assortment of interesting bones of creatures which had lived long, long ago. And each new find convinced me more and more that the Bible did not give the correct account of the creation. It was not until years later, when I knew much more about the Bible, and much more about science too, that the mystery was solved for me. Some of you may have hunted for fossils, or perhaps you have learned more about the earliest times of the world than I did at school, and so you may have the same feeling of doubt about the Bible as I had. If so, you'll probably want, just as I did, to know why it is that the Bible seems to start off with what appears to be a fairy-tale.

2: THE BOOK THAT IS DIFFERENT

The Bible is a strange book. Most books are written by one author, who just sits down and writes and writes and writes until he finishes it, but the Bible was written by lots of different people. Of course there are other books which are written by a lot of people; encyclopedias for instance, in which the articles about the different subjects may be written by dozens or even hundreds of people all with special little bits of knowledge. But the Bible is not like this either, because an encyclopedia is all written at more or less the same time whereas the various authors whose work is in the Bible lived at very different times.

Actually the Bible is a collection of all sorts of different bits of writing, some of which are as much as a thousand years older than others. The various bits were not all written in the same language, though nowadays we read it all in English translations. About the only way in which all the bits are alike is that they are all about God—God creating the world, God at work in history, God telling people what was right and what was wrong, and so on.

And it was written by people. Often they were very learned people, but they were people just the same, and not a collection of dictation machines recording the word of God with one-hundred-per-cent efficiency. And it was other people too who selected the writings and put them together to form the Bible a long time ago, and still other people who copied the manuscripts by hand throughout the early centuries, and others again who edited them and translated them into Latin and English and German and French, and later into Rarotongan and Motu and a thousand other little-known languages.

When I was at school I did not realize this. I thought of the Bible as a single book, and I never really thought about where it came from. Nor did I realize that a lot of it was poetry. Obviously the psalms were poetry of a kind, but nobody ever explained to me that much of the rest is poetry too, although it has lost the appearance of poetry through being translated.

Poets are strange people. They don't write a simple, straightforward account of things in the way that a newspaper reporter does, because they are concerned with the beauty in things, and the feelings that things bring to them, feelings of great happiness, or despair, or trust, or hope, or disappointment. To do this they often say the oddest things to help to express what they feel. The English poet Shelley wrote of the skylark:—'Hail to thee, blithe spirit, *bird thou never wert.*' We know perfectly well what he meant, but if we just take the words as they stand his statement is untrue. If a skylark is not a bird, what is?

Then there is the poem 'To Celia' by Ben Jonson. 'Drink to me only with thine eyes . . .' We know perfectly well that we see with our eyes and drink with our mouths, but the poet can paint a picture for us with his words so that we can understand what he means. Even I myself am writing like a poet just now, because of course it is really artists and not poets who *paint pictures.*

In reading the Bible we must always try to understand what the writer *means* rather than what he *says,* because it was the meaning that was so important to him, whether he was describing his own experiences of God or merely recording tales which had come down from generation to generation for hundreds of years.

The Bible opens with the story of the creation which worried me as a boy. It says nothing about the *Ichthyosaurus,* but it says a great deal about the creation of the whole world and the stars and the parts of the universe beyond our reach. In fact this first bit of the Bible is called 'Genesis,' a word which means the 'making' or 'creation,' and it sets out to tell how God made the world, and where men and women came from. There are several ideas about the same thing mixed up together, and right at the beginning of Genesis there are two stories about how the Earth was made, and how all the living things came to live upon it. The second of these two stories, which begins in the middle of Chapter 2, verse 4, is some three or four hundred years older than the one on the first page, and it does not tell us nearly as much.

The account of the 'creation' at the beginning of Genesis was written about 2,400 years ago. In those days there were no microscopes to see very tiny things, no electron microscopes to see even smaller ones, no telescopes to look at the Moon and stars, none of the wonderful gadgets that we can use today to find out about so many things. And if you lived in those days and wondered what the Earth and the sky were really like and how they were put together, or why the stars were always in the same patterns, the only thing to do was to look at them day after day and night after night and try to solve the puzzle.

Now the curious thing is that many things are not what they seem to be when you look at them in this way. For instance, if you climb up to the top of a hill and look over the countryside at the fields and villages, and even at the sea, you are certain to think that it all looks flat. At the same time you

know perfectly well that it is not flat but curved, because it is really part of the surface of an enormous round ball, the Earth.

Probably you have never bothered to ask yourself *how* you know that the Earth is round and not flat. The answer is that your geography teachers, and perhaps your parents too, have always told you so, and you just believed what they told you —quite rightly, because they were telling the facts as they had learned them, and these were the truth. But even your teachers only know that the Earth is round because they have read about it, and seen pictures in books. They have not actually sailed around the world to find out. They are passing on true facts which were *proved* to be true over four hundred years ago when Magellan first actually sailed around the Earth—though various people in different parts of the world had thought at various times as far back as 650 B.C. that the Earth might be round. When your teachers tell you things, they are nearly always telling you what other people

have discovered. This is quite natural, and no school teachers feel that they should travel all the way to the poles to make certain that there are penguins in the Antarctic and polar bears in the Arctic, nor fly off in a rocket to make sure that there really are rings around the planet Saturn, nor be bitten by a Mamba in the African jungle in order to be able to tell you that it is a particularly poisonous African snake. Other people have discovered these things, and have passed on their knowledge. Eventually it reaches you through your teachers, or parents, or books, which are just passing on the discoveries of everybody all over the world.

But a long time ago the people who tried to think about things were not so lucky as you, because they had to find out everything for themselves. There was hardly any information passed down from other people, and even the little there was did not turn out to be very accurate. And so, as a result, they sometimes explained things wrongly, just as nowadays we find that professors and scientists as well as other people, when they are trying to solve some new puzzle about which nothing is already known for certain, report things which a few years later turn out to be wrong.

For instance, everybody has always known that if meat is left out in the air it eventually comes to be full of maggots, so it was natural enough for people of old to think that rotten meat actually turned into maggots. It was quite a long time before scientists discovered that this old idea was wrong, and that the maggots appeared because flies had laid their eggs on the meat, and the eggs had hatched into maggots.

We always expect science to give us a greater knowledge of things of this kind, and so we should not be surprised to find that some of the things which Genesis tells us about the way in which the universe is put together are different from what we know nowadays. But people seem to forget this, and often they are puzzled—just as I was as a boy—that the Bible seems to contain mistakes. They forget that nowadays we have all sorts of wonderful inventions which help us to find out about the stars and the sun, or the microscopic creatures which live in the sea. Instead of feeling puzzled we should stop and consider how wonderful it is that men who lived about two thousand four hundred years ago could know as much as they did. And we should always remember one thing more—and that is, that there are many things we ourselves still do not know, even in these days of wonderful inventions.

3: DARKNESS AND WATER

The first chapter of Genesis was written some 2,400 years ago, and it would not say much for our science if we knew nothing more about the universe than the man who wrote about it so long ago. If we take his description of the creation we can now fill some of the gaps in his story with the discoveries which have been made during the many centuries since it was written. The Genesis story begins like this:—

In the beginning God created the heavens and the earth.

It does not say when 'the beginning' was. The date 4004 B.C. printed at the top of the page in some editions of the Bible was not put there by the Genesis writer. It was added by an Irish archbishop in the seventeenth century. And we still have no very clear idea of when the beginning was, but we know that many of the stars are at least four thousand million years old, and that the Earth is rather newer — probably about three thousand million years. This seems such a long period of time that you may think it is just a wild guess, but it is not. We can be fairly certain about it. Some of the rocks in our mountains contain rare metals, such as uranium, which are very slowly turning into lead, and always have been. By determining how much of the metal has already turned into lead we can work out roughly how long the rocks must have been there. In this way it has been found out that the Earth is at least three thousand million years of age, and possibly even older. Even my *Ichthyosaurus* bones were quite new compared with the age of the Earth.

The Genesis writer says that in this far off beginning God created the heavens and the Earth. We no longer use the word 'heavens' for the objects that we can see in the night sky, but we talk instead of the 'universe'—which really means the 'everything,' and when we talk of the universe we mean the same as he did when he wrote of the heavens and the Earth. Just how the universe was created we do not really know. Nor did the man who wrote the Genesis story, and he was sensible enough not to try to say anything about it. But it was quite obvious to him that the universe was a most wonderful thing and could not possibly have been made by accident. Although he lived more than two thousand years ago he had no doubt at all that it was made by God. Nothing else could account for it. From end to end it was full of power and beauty and magnificent design, and he saw the universe as a wonderful example of God's cleverness and power in making things. Einstein, one of the greatest of our modern scientists, said exactly the same thing, and all the wonderful telescopes in the modern observatories seem to confirm what the Genesis writer said so long ago—that the universe was obviously the work of God.

Of course the universe may have been made all in a flash, or it may have been created very slowly, little by little. Although we still do not know for certain, this slow process of creation seems to be the most likely way. Some scientists think that atoms (the smallest possible particles) of a gas called hydrogen are continually being created all through the universe, and that after many millions of years they eventually build up the stars which we can see in the sky.

If you ask how these new atoms are created, and from what they are made, the answer is that we do not know as yet just what happens, but it seems that the new material is not made from anything else. It is just made. In fact it is 'created.'

If we know very little about the creation of the universe, we do not know very much more about the beginnings of the Earth itself. One reasonable idea is that there was once a star which moved around the Sun a long way from it. The star exploded, leaving behind a great mass of material, and this stuff gradually became clumped together into a great big mass which became unsteady and broke up into pieces, one bit forming the Earth and others forming the other smaller ones among the family of planets which travel around the Sun. All this is really guesswork, and although some of our modern astronomers who study stars are surprisingly good at making right guesses about this kind of thing, in another thousand years some of their ideas may seem very unusual indeed, just as one or two of the Genesis ideas seem rather strange to us today.

The earth was without form and void,

The Earth was without form—that is, it had no definite shape; there was nothing about it which could really be described.

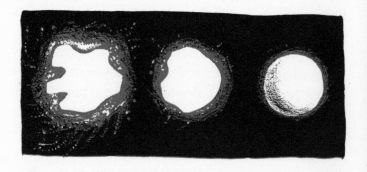

When the mass of material broke up to form the Earth and the other small planets it must have been extremely hot, quite as hot as the hottest blast furnaces which you could find in steel works anywhere in the world today. In fact it must have been so hot that the rocks were not hard and stony, but soft and sticky, perhaps as runny as molasses or syrup. When the big mass broke up, the frag-

16

ments which came to form the Earth and the other planets must quickly have become round in shape, like enormous balls, the weight or 'gravity' of each piece pulling it into a shape at which each bit of the surface was about the same distance from the center. And this shape, if you come to think of it, is bound to be that of a ball. So the Earth, from having no definite shape, came to be round. 'Void' means empty, and the Genesis writer meant that there was nothing alive on it, no birds or animals, no fishes, no men. This must certainly have been true, because the Earth was much too hot for any living thing to survive upon it. There is no living thing which can stand the temperature of a kitchen oven—and the Earth must at first have been at least ten or twenty times as hot as that. Not even the snakes which live in the hot deserts can stand the heat of the Sun for more than a very few minutes. If they cannot burrow into a shady hole they quickly die. Another reason why there could not be any life was that at that time there was no water to be found on the Earth. The water had not yet formed. All living things on the Earth have a great deal of water inside their bodies, and so they must have been formed later than the water which they contain. Even creatures which live in the driest deserts have water in all the cells of their bodies.

We know that the Earth must have existed for thousands of centuries before there was any life on it, because the oldest remains of living things are less than one third of the age of the Earth.

17

The Genesis writer may have guessed that the Earth was uninhabited in the beginning, but it seems to have been a good guess.

And darkness was upon the face of the deep;

We usually think of the 'deep' as a huge expanse of water like the Atlantic Ocean, and it seems that the Genesis writer thought very much the same. But his 'deep' was not the same as ours. He thought of the deep as a great mass of water *underneath* the Earth, while we think of it as the water lying on the surface of the Earth and separating the continents. But this ocean deep of ours is 'the waters under the heavens' which, as we shall see, come rather later in the Genesis story.

No, the 'deep' of Genesis was not the ocean. It was a mysterious mass of water which was there before the land was formed at all, according to the story. The Genesis writer thought that the water was there first and that somehow the dry land appeared out of it, but this was not the way it happened. From what we can work out about the early history of the Earth we can be certain that the dry land was there first and that the oceans (our kind of 'deep,' and not his) appeared much later.

It was probably not until two thousand million years after the formation of the Earth that the immense masses of water in the oceans appeared, and we can work out fairly accurately the steps which must have led up to the arrival of all this water upon an Earth which previously had been dry and hot.

At first the surface of the Earth must have been so hot that it was molten, but it must have cooled fairly quickly until a crust of solid rock was formed on the surface. Probably the formation of this crust took only a few thousand years at the most. This skin would slow down the cooling, just as a layer of wrapping around a hot-water tank will help to preserve its heat, and so the skin of the Earth remained hot and fairly thin for a long while. As the Earth went on slowly cooling it shrank, and the skin was forced into wrinkles like those on the skin of an apple as it shrinks in the cupboard.

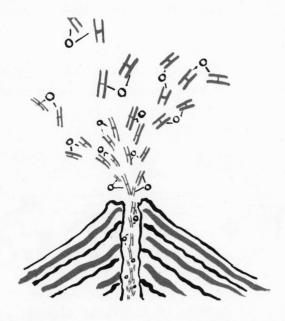

These wrinkles were the first mountain ranges— other mountains were formed much later by further shrinkings and upheavals. Now at last the familiar outlines of the world were beginning to take shape.

Weak spots in the surface skin of the Earth broke, and molten rock came bubbling up, like the milk that bubbles through holes in the skin of a rice pudding. These holes were volcanoes, and there used to be many thousands of them on the surface of the Earth, although today there are only a few really active ones—such as Vesuvius and Etna in Europe, and Popocatapetl in Mexico. Quite a number of our mountains and hills were once volcanoes, and the great water-filled pit at Crater Lake in Oregon was once a magnificent volcano, visible for hundreds of miles at night.

Enormous quantities of gas bubbled out of the thousands of volcanoes, and nearly all of it was hydrogen, a gas which burns fiercely in air. About one fifth of the air is oxygen, and two atoms of hydrogen will burn with one of oxygen to form a particle of water:

$$2H + O \longrightarrow H_2O$$

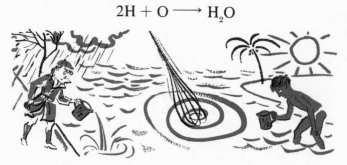

These tiny particles or 'molecules' of water are incredibly small. If you were to take a tumbler of water and pour it into the sea, and if all the seas and oceans were thoroughly stirred up so that your original tumbler of water was dispersed through-

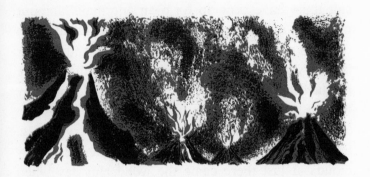

out the Atlantic, the Pacific, and the Indian Ocean, and into all the bays and inlets right around the world, you could go down to the shore anywhere in the world and dip your tumbler into the sea again, and be certain that you were trapping at least seventy of the water molecules from your original half pint of water. This gives some idea of the vast number of water molecules in the oceans, and the huge quantities of hydrogen atoms which must have issued from the volcanoes in order to form them. For it is to the volcanoes that we owe every drop of the water in the world today.

Our few remaining active volcanoes are still manufacturing water. If you lived in Italy you could still sometimes see the hydrogen burning at the top of Vesuvius, and you would see a great cloud drifting away in the wind beyond the flame. This cloud is not smoke, but steam, because when the hydrogen unites with the oxygen in the air it forms steam—which is just water in a heated state. In the early days of the Earth there must have been thousands of volcanoes belching flame as they shot out their hydrogen to burn in the air, and the re-

21

sult must have been to form an enormous amount of steam or cloud. All the while, as the millions of years passed, the clouds grew thicker and thicker but they never fell as rain. So long as the surface of the Earth was still hot, no rain could possibly fall.

Yet all the while the Earth was cooling very slowly, and after some twenty thousand centuries of steamy clouds at last there came the wonderful day when the rain first fell upon the dry, rocky, crinkled surface of our Earth beneath. It must have been absolutely dark upon the Earth at the time, the clouds being so thick that no ray of light could shine through them. And when the rain began to fall it came down in sheets, day after day, and week after week.

Most of us have experienced a long, heavy rain-storm when everything seemed to be running with water, but the worst we may have seen is hardly a drop in the bucket compared with the storm that led to the formation of the 'deep.' Almost all the water on our Earth today fell in that first great downpour, and it has been worked out from the amount of water on the Earth that this first great rain probably lasted for something like forty thousand years without a break.

And as the rain fell year after year, century after century, it ran down the mountainsides, washing away stones and pieces of rock, tearing ever onward towards the lowest portions of the Earth's surface, there to form the seas, the oceans, the 'deep' of our world today.

4: THE STRANGE DOME

And the spirit of God was moving over the face of the deep; And God said, "Let there be light"; and there was light.

For many millions of years the absolute darkness of the dense layer of clouds had shrouded the Earth in blackness. Then at last came the glorious day when the great rain drew towards its close, and the brilliant sunshine shone through rifts in the clouds upon the land and water beneath. It must have been a wonderful sight, and it is sad to think that there was at that moment no living thing upon the Earth to see the beauty of that first day of sunshine after the countless centuries of darkness.

The Earth, basking in the new sunshine, must have looked very different from today. In the first place the colors would have been quite different. There would have been no green (for there were no plants), no brown earthy soil (which is made from dead plants), no white chalk cliffs (which are built

from the remains of minute creatures which did
not exist)—nothing in fact but the brilliant colors
of rocks and the sharp, reddish peaks sticking up
above the valleys cut by the torrents and rivers
of fallen rain, and at the edge of the land masses
a sea of incredible brightness and blueness. No
sea-weed was growing in it as yet, no boats were
dumping refuse among the waves, no great tankers
were discharging waste oil. The whole world was
bright and clear as crystal—and absolutely silent
but for the wind whistling around the rocky cliffs
and the splashing of torrents and waterfalls. It was
a world which simply lacked one thing to make it
perfect in its beauty. And that missing thing was
life.

Life was soon to appear. But before we discover
what forms were to appear on the Earth we must
see how the Genesis writer goes on to give a description of the Earth and the way he fits it into the
rest of the universe.

*And God saw that the light was good; and God
separated the light from the darkness. And God
called the light Day, and the darkness he called
Night. And there was evening and there was morning, one day. And God said, "Let there be a firmament in the midst of the waters, and let it separate
the waters from the waters." And God made the
firmament and separated the waters which were
under the firmament from the waters which were
above the firmament. And it was so. And God
called the firmament Heaven.*

This description needs explaining, if only because the word 'firmament' is one which we never use nowadays. The clue to its meaning is in the first four letters, 'firm.' A firmament was something firm, something broad and wide, a kind of roof or covering like a huge glass dome.

The easiest way to see how people thought about the Earth and sky two thousand years ago is to go out on a clear night and look around over the surrounding countryside. Glance up into the sky, and look at what is there as though it were something you had never seen before. If you do this you will see what the Genesis writer saw, and you might easily describe it in the fine way in which he described it, if you thought about it carefully.

Try to forget for a moment all that you have learned at school or from books about the Earth being a planet revolving around the Sun, and about the stars being other suns far away in space, some of them much closer than others. All this is perfectly true, but we have only discovered it through centuries of patient work. If we are to see the universe as the Genesis writer saw it we have to think of the Earth as being the center of everything with the rest of the universe all arranged around it for some useful purpose—useful, that is, to us on the Earth.

If you put yourself in the position of the writer of this first chapter of Genesis, what you can see is the countryside all in darkness, apparently part of an enormous piece of land which runs on and on until you come to the sea. The land may have hills here and there, but otherwise it is flat. Overhead there seems to be a huge roof like a bowl turned upside down, and in it the stars appear to be set like jewels, twinkling brightly.

A man looking at this same beautiful night scene two thousand years ago would have asked himself several questions. First of all, why was it that if he threw a stone up into the air it fell down to the ground, but the stars did not fall out of the sky? Surely the answer could only be that something kept the stars up. They seemed to be hanging on something, stuck like overhead lamps in a far-away roof. Perhaps there really was a roof—a firmament.

Then there would be the curious fact that the sky was a kind of very dark blackish blue at night, but in the daytime it was light blue. The same thing was true of lakes and the sea. They too were dark blue at night and light blue by day. Nowadays we know that most of this color is merely reflected from the sky, but an equally sensible explanation might have been that up beyond the sky there was a great mass of water, and it was this which gave the color to the heavens above.

But if there was all this water up above the Earth, why did it not fall down? It too must surely be kept in place by something, but it could hardly be hanging on the underneath of the firmament as the stars were. A reasonable explanation of this was that the water was on the far side of the firmament, and that the firmament or dome was transparent so that you could see the water through it. If the stars were on one side and the water on the other, this would explain why the water did not put out the light of the stars.

Then there was the equally strange fact that although the Earth seemed to be just a flat plate, the water in the sea did not run off at the edges and disappear, but remained piled up against the coasts and islands. Something was obviously keeping it in. There might be a wall at the edge of the flat Earth—but why bother about a wall? If there was a firmament, the firmament must be supported on something, and presumably it came down to the edge of the Earth all the way around, like a glass cover over a plate of sandwiches.

So the one obvious solution which answered all these awkward questions and which explained what seemed to be there at night was a 'firmament,' a great transparent roof, with water covering it on the far side. The stars were fixed on the underneath side of the firmament, and around the edge of the Earth the firmament came right down to the bottom of the sea. In fact, if you were an adventurous kind of person in a boat you might sail to the far side of the sea, and when you got there you would bump into the firmament where it came down around the water to stop it all from falling away over the edge of the Earth.

If you can look at the sky and see it in the way the Genesis writer saw it, you can understand why he wrote of several different kinds of water. There were the 'waters above the firmament,' the vast

27

mass of water lying beyond the clear roof, the water which gave the color to the sky. Some of this occasionally fell down as rain—which only went to prove that the water was there. The man two thousand years ago naturally thought that there must be holes or trap doors in the firmament which could be opened to let the rain fall through. If you read the story of Noah you will see that God was believed to turn the rain on and off by opening and stopping up these 'windows of heaven.' Nowadays we have our great telescopes and we know that the firmament is not there at all, and we know that there is no huge mass of water lying up in the sky ready to drop through the windows or skylights. We also know a little bit more about how rain is formed, although we cannot explain the whole process as well as we should like to.

Rain is not new water (except near volcanoes), but old water that returns to earth. Water vapor is continuously being taken up by the air from the sea, the lakes and the rivers. By and by the air becomes full or 'saturated' and will take up no more. This air rises like hot air going up a chimney until it is high in the sky where the temperature is much colder. Now warm air will hold much more water than cold air and so when the warm air is cooled down, high up in the sky, it loses some of the water which is turned loose as tiny droplets to form a cloud.

Clouds are also formed when air is made to rise for other reasons. If you have ever lived or visited among the mountains you will know how a high peak often has a curious patch of cloud sitting on its top, stretching away downwind like smoke from a factory chimney. It looks very much as though the top of the mountain is giving out a cloud as a volcano does, but the reason for this kind of cloud is quite different. Air saturated with water vapor blows across the land and when it reaches the slopes of the mountain it is forced upwards to flow over the top. As it goes upward it expands, because there is not quite so much other air sitting on it and squashing it as there was when it was passing over the lower country.

As saturated air expands, it gets cooler and it cannot hold all its water. The surplus water gathers in little droplets and that is what forms the clouds over the mountain tops.

The drops in a cloud are too small to fall as rain, and they hang in the sky until the air becomes so cold that some of them become tiny, sharp crystals of ice. When this happens, the water droplets run together very quickly and as soon as they are heavy enough they fall as rain.

Sometimes, when clouds have hung over the land for a long time without dropping any rain, people have made the rain fall by scattering dry ice powder on the clouds from an airplane or by firing shells containing silver iodide smoke, which consists of very small and sharp particles. In one experiment a rainstorm covering forty-five square miles was made by scattering twenty-five pounds of dry ice from a plane. But on other occasions the experiment did not work, which only goes to show that there is still a lot we do not know about why rain falls from some clouds and not from others. If we knew the whole story, then our weather forecasts on the radio would be more correct than they are at the moment, and they would no longer warn us of rain which never appears, or promise a fine week-end so that we leave our raincoats at home and get soaked to the skin.

So the 'waters above the firmament' were thought to be the big mass of water which gave the sky its color and provided the rain. But they were not the only waters mentioned in the Genesis story. There were the 'waters under the firmament,' or the 'deep.' These, as we have already seen, were supposed to be great masses of water underneath the Earth, and the reason why the Earth did not sink in them was because it was believed to be held up on a lot of pillars, like a pier at the lake or the seashore. The man who wrote the Genesis story did not worry about what these pillars rested on, just as you can sit comfortably on a pier without wondering whether the supports are set in concrete or driven into the mud. The pillars are not mentioned in the Genesis story, but you can find them mentioned in the book of Job (chapters 9 and 26), and Psalm 24 shows the idea of the Earth being held up above the water in the same way:—'The earth is the Lord's. . . . he hath *founded it upon the seas,* and established it upon the floods.'

And there was evening and there was morning, a second day.

30

Nowadays we know that the creation was not done in a few days, but we see it as a long process covering vast ages of time. The Genesis writer may have thought that the whole creation was completed in a week, because he was so tremendously impressed with God's skill in making things. However it seems much more likely that this is just the poet's habit of saying things in a striking way, and that he meant 'ages,' not days of twenty-four hours; just as Isaac Watts in the eighteenth century wrote his well-known lines:

> 'A thousand ages in Thy sight
> Are like an evening gone.'

Nowadays we know for certain that the 'creation' covered millions of years, and the way in which it took place in such a careful and beautiful way strikes us as very wonderful. The forming of the Earth, the slow cooling until the rain fell, the appearance of life—each of these was a milestone in the long history of the Earth, and though these milestones are separated by millions of years they all point slowly but surely in the same direction.

And God said, "Let the waters under the heavens be gathered together into one place, and let the dry land appear." And it was so. God called the dry land Earth, and the waters that were gathered together he called Seas. And God saw that it was good.

Here is our third and last kind of water, and this time it is real enough. It is not imaginary like the waters above the firmament or the waters under the Earth. These waters are our seas and oceans, which we have already seen to have been mostly formed in one great downpour.

The Genesis writer does not tell us in this story where the seawater came from but there are hints in other Bible writings. The general idea seems to have been that they came from the mythical 'deep' underneath the Earth, by way of springs.

No doubt you have been told about springs in your geography lessons at school. Rain seeps through the ground and runs through a porous layer of rock until it reaches a hard layer which prevents it from sinking any further. It then has to flow along the surface of this layer until it finds an exit, often on a hill side. And where it comes out it forms a spring.

There are some fine springs in the United States and in Canada, usually in limestone. But one of the best I have ever seen is in the village of Ashwell in England. This spring is so large that the whole River Cam comes rushing out of it at the bottom of a little rocky cliff in the middle of the village. When I first saw it I remembered at once what I had been taught about springs at school. But if I had been living a couple of thousand years ago and nobody had told me how the water came to be rushing out of the rocks I might have had very different ideas—particularly if I had thought that the whole Earth was only a thin, flat plate resting on pillars sunk in the 'deep.' I might easily have thought that it was the water from below, which was spouting out of the ground. I might even have called springs by the name which is given to them in Genesis Chapter 7—'fountains of the deep.'

If you have ever been on a pier at a seaside or lakeside on a rough day you will understand very easily the idea of the 'waters under the heaven' coming up from below. As the sea splashes against the pillars of the pier, jets of water come splashing through the boards, leaving little pools on the pier.

The first oceans, formed by the torrents of the first great storm, were very much in the same places as they are today, but not exactly. Through millions of years waves washing against the coasts have altered the shapes of the continents, and the shrinking of the Earth and the continued wrinkling of its surface have flooded areas of land once dry, and raised up hills that were once the floor of the

sea. The chalk works of west Kansas and the cement quarries of Pennsylvania are both places which millions of years ago were at the bottom of the sea. And in Europe only ten thousand years ago you could have walked from England to France without getting your feet wet.

In some places the sea is slowly eating away at the coast. When I was quite small I was taken to stay in a house which stood some way back from the edge of the cliffs, and I used to cross a field to reach the path that led down to the water. Twelve years afterwards I happened to see the house again. It was now about six yards from the edge of the cliff, and a hopeful notice on the gate said that it was for sale. A year or two later the house had vanished.

When I found that the scene of my childhood holidays had gone, I realized very clearly the way in which the areas of land and sea are continually and slowly shifting year by year. I no longer found it quite so surprising that I should have picked up the bones of a great marine reptile right out in the country, a hundred miles from the coast.

5: THE EARTH GOES GREEN

And God said, "Let the earth put forth vegetation, plants yielding seed, and fruit trees bearing fruit in which is their seed, each according to its kind, upon the earth." And it was so. The earth brought forth vegetation, plants yielding seed according to their own kinds, and trees bearing fruit in which is their seed, each according to its kind. And God saw that it was good. And there was evening and there was morning, a third day.

Like the Genesis author in his time, we of today can see all the different kinds of plants which cover the surface of the land, but we have an advantage over him because we now have quarries and coal mines to study. If we look at the stones dug out of them we can sometimes find the remains or fossils of plants which lived a very long time ago, and which are no longer to be seen alive anywhere on the Earth. If we look carefully and figure the ages of the remains we dig up, we can work out

35

that the very first live things probably appeared on earth just about one thousand million years ago. We can only guess what those first living things were, although we are certain that they were so very small they would not have left any remains for us to dig up. Probably they were something like germs, only smaller and simpler. However that may be, they were probably the ancestors not only of every kind of plant found on the Earth today, but of every animal too. Even of ourselves.

We can be quite certain that life began in the water, and that for about the next five hundred million years all living things remained in the water. It was a long time before any living creature, whether a plant or an animal, grew a skin tough enough for it to be able to live on land without the risk of being dried up by the sunshine in the way a jellyfish is shriveled up if it is thrown on the beach by a wave.

Slowly, as day succeeded day and spring followed winter, the wonderful process of life went on. The first live creatures lived, and as the millions of years flowed by they were replaced by more and more separate kinds, which were at the same time larger and more complicated. Five hundred million years ago there were sea-weeds, and these in turn went on through the ages to be the ancestors of mosses and ferns. Plants were slowly managing to grow further up from the seas in bogs and on the beaches, and the huge horse-tails which grew in swamps two hundred and fifty million years ago lay where they died, and slowly turned into the coal which we burn today. The small horse-tails which we find in the woods today are the only survivors of the plants of those distant times.

I never sit beside a coal fire on a winter's evening without a strange feeling that time has disappeared, and that I am in touch with those queer plants which grew so far back in the past, the remains of which are now glowing brightly in my grate. Millions of centuries ago their leaves stored the energy of the bright sunlight, and laid up a store of fuel in the coal fields. As I gaze into the flickering flames I seem to be wandering through the hot, steamy swamps, picking my way over the fallen trunks of strange plant giants. And when the coal splits with a crack in the heat of the fire I seem to hear the crash as yet another huge tree thunders into the debris below, scattering the great dragonflies as it falls.

After the coal forests came the pine trees with their cones and needles, and at last, less than a hundred million years ago, the first plants with beautiful flowers began to grow upon the Earth. Little by little the lovely flowers of our hills and streams and woods came to brighten the Earth with their gay colors and fill the summer air with their scent just as they do today.

6: OUT INTO SPACE

And God said, "Let there be lights in the firmament of the heavens to separate the day from the night; and let them be for signs and for seasons and for days and years, and let them be lights in the firmament of the heavens to give light upon the earth." And it was so.

This part of the story should really come at the beginning since it tells about the Sun. But two thousand years ago people thought of the Earth as the center of everything in the universe, and so the story naturally began with the Earth. For several hundred years it has been known that the Earth travels around the Sun, whirling through space in a great wide course or 'orbit' at a distance of about ninety-three million miles from it. We can be certain that the Sun was there long before the Earth was formed, and not the other way around. Year in and year out the Earth runs along its invisible track around the Sun. If you work out the speed at which it must be traveling in order to cover such a huge circle once every year, you will find that it is moving through space at about sixty thousand miles per hour, a speed which makes our best modern airplanes seem quite slow.

All the while, the Earth is spinning around as it goes; and all the while, half of it is in the sunshine while the other half is in the dark, turned away from the Sun. At sunrise the part of the surface where you live is just turning into the sunshine, and at sunset it is turning away again.

Most people think that the Earth turns completely around once in every twenty-four hours, but they are mistaken. Actually the time taken for the Earth to spin around once is twenty-three hours and fifty-six minutes. But by the time it has turned completely around it has also moved a little further along its yearly orbit around the Sun, and it has to turn a little bit further before the same part is facing exactly opposite the sun again. This little extra bit of turning takes four minutes, so that it is twenty-three hours and fifty-six minutes, plus four minutes, before exactly the same side of the Earth is turned towards the Sun. This is why our 'days' are twenty-four hours long although the Earth takes a few minutes less than twenty-four hours to turn around.

But it has not always been so. When the Earth was first formed, a day was only about four hours long, because the Earth was turning much more quickly. It has been slowed down to its present speed of turning by the Moon, which acts as a kind of brake.

Ever since the beginning the days have been getting longer, and they will continue to get longer and longer as the years roll by, although the difference will not really be enough to notice. After another million years each of our days will only be a few seconds longer than it is now.

We measure our days and hours and years by the motion of the Earth, and it is strange to realize that if it were not moving we might be quite unable to tell what the time was, or even when a year had passed. Nor for that matter should we have any seasons. There would be no summer heatwaves giving way in winter to frost and snow and days of skiing and sledding and skating. Instead we would have only a flat and dull climate, always the same all through the year.

The seasons are not due just to the fact that the Earth spins. They are caused by its spinning at an angle, so that one pole is pointed slightly towards the Sun and the other pole slightly away from it. This affects the amount of sunlight which falls on either end. Each half of the Earth receives rather more than a twelve-hour share of daylight when pointing towards the Sun, but rather less when pointing away from it. In spring and autumn the north and south halves receive the same amount of sunlight, but in what we call 'summer,' the United States and Canada and Europe (which are all in the northern half) receive a larger share, while Australia (which is in the southern half) gets only a little sunshine. So it is 'winter' in Australia when it is summer with us. Six months later the seasons are the other way around and we have only a short day in the winter while Australians enjoy their summer sunshine and play cricket in December.

So night and day, the seasons and the passing of the years are all due to the particular way in which the Earth moves around the Sun.

And God made the two great lights, the greater light to rule the day, and the lesser light to rule the night.

The 'greater light' is of course the Sun and the 'lesser light' the Moon. We know more about the Moon than any other part of the universe outside the Earth, partly because it is so much closer to us. Although it is a quarter of a million miles away, this is only about one three hundred and sixtieth part of the distance to the Sun.

The Moon is much smaller than the Earth and it moves around us, taking just under four weeks to complete the circle. It does not shine of its own accord but reflects the bright light of the Sun, just as a signpost shines in the brilliance of the head-light of a car. The same side of the Moon is always facing toward the Earth, and so we have never been able to see the other side. But it would be a fair guess that it is much the same as the side we can see.

There is no life on the Moon. It is cold and dry, and without any air. It has been so constantly bom-barded by large rocks or 'meteors'—that the surface is covered with huge holes or dents, some of them more than a hundred miles from side to side.

The Earth too would be struck by showers of rocks in just the same way if it were not for the air which surrounds it. This air burns up the meteors on their way down, so that they nearly always disappear as streaks of light or 'shooting stars' before reaching the ground.

The Moon may have been formed at the same time as the Earth, from the breaking up of a great mass of material from the explosion of an old star. Or it may once have been part of the Earth. It certainly seems possible that it was flung off the Earth not long after our world was first formed, and when it was still soft.

There seems to be a pit in the surface of the Earth which is just about the right size to be the place from which the Moon was thrown off into space. This hole is now full of water, and forms the Pacific Ocean, but we may never know for certain whether or not this was the place from which the Moon came. Voyages to the Moon are no longer the wild fancy they once seemed, but anyone making the trip will certainly find it a dull place compared with the Earth, and will be glad to get home again.

The Sun is more important to us than anything else in the whole universe. Its strong pull holds the Earth on its right course, and most of its terrific heat is fortunately shut off from us by the whirling layers of its surface. More than eight hundred and sixty thousand miles across, the Sun is so hot in its center that if you could put a shovelful of Sun on the top of the Empire State Building, everything in the whole of New York City and as far west as Nebraska or Kansas would be scorched and burned by the heat of it.

The Sun is about seven thousand times as hot as the very best furnaces in factories, so hot that we cannot begin to imagine it. But strangely enough the Sun is not burning, in spite of its terrific heat. The immense heat is almost certainly made by atoms of hydrogen gas joining together to form another gas called 'helium.' This process happens slowly, but it is accompanied by the most tremendous output of heat and light, and even at a distance of ninety-three million miles the roof of your house receives as much heating from the Sun every day as would be provided by about a quarter of a ton of coke burned in the furnace.

Not only does the Sun provide heat and light, but the very air we breathe depends upon it. Plants take in carbon dioxide from the air, and use the energy from the sunlight to convert this into sugars,

¼ ton of coke

and starch, and the other materials which are stored in their leaves and stems. What they really do is take out the carbon atoms and keep them, returning the oxygen to the air again.

The plants could not exist without sunlight, nor could we. This is partly because we ourselves, and all the other animals, depend in the long run upon plants for our food, and also because we breathe the oxygen in the air and breathe out carbon dioxide in return. The plants perform a valuable service to us in taking our carbon dioxide out of the air, and returning the oxygen for us to breathe once more.

Without the supply of energy from the Sun none of this could happen, and there could be no life at all upon the Earth. The Genesis writer did not know this, or he would certainly have pointed out the wonderful use of the Sun for every living thing upon the Earth.

Instead, he goes on to tell how he thought God arranged the stars, and how they were held up in the sky.

He made the stars also. And God set them in the firmament of the heavens to give light upon the earth, to rule over the day and over the night, and to separate the light from the darkness. And God saw that it was good. And there was evening and there was morning, a fourth day.

The stars which we see in the sky at night are not all the same distance from the Earth, set on the surface of a glassy dome as the Genesis writer thought. They are spread about for immense distances into space. The farthest groups of them which can be seen with our magnificent telescopes are about fifteen hundred million million million miles away from us—a distance which is so immense that we cannot even begin to imagine it.

Light travels so fast that it could flash seven times around the world in a second. It moves so quickly that although the Moon is a quarter of a million miles away from us a lighthouse flashing on the Moon would be seen on the Earth only one and a third seconds after it had flashed. But the stars are so far away that the light from the closest one takes well over four years to reach us on the Earth. The light now reaching us from the most distant groups which our telescopes reveal to us left them over three hundred million years ago, long before the giant horse-tails and ferns of the swamps were rotting to form our coal long ago. Sometimes we see a star explode, but the explosion has happened many years before we see it. The flash has been traveling towards us for a long time as it crossed the huge distance separating us from the star, to be seen at last by us here on the Earth.
Some of the stars are huge, and some small, but one that looks large in the sky may not be as big as one that appears very small and faint. It very much depends on how close they are to us, and a small one close to us—if one can call twenty-six million million miles 'close' at all—may look bigger

45

than a giant star a thousand times as far away. We only know their real size by the careful and patient work of astronomers. Compared with the Sun, some of the stars are small, but others are as large as the Yankee Stadium compared with a baseball.

We only see the stars at night, but they are there in the daytime just the same. It is just that the light of the Sun makes the sky too bright for us to see them. Though we do not usually realize it, our own Sun is one of the countless stars, and it only looks so much larger and brighter because it is much closer to us than the others. It is only one three hundred thousandth part of the distance away from us of the nearest of all the other myriad stars.

7: EGGS IN PLENTY

And God said, "Let the waters bring forth swarms of living creatures, and let birds fly above the earth across the firmament of the heavens." So God created the great sea monsters and every living creature that moves, with which the waters swarm, according to their kinds, and every winged bird according to its kind. And God saw that it was good.

So far as we can tell, the animals and plants shared the same ancestors at the beginning of life in the waters, but shortly afterwards they began to go their different ways. It took five hundred million years to produce the first animals several inches long—sea-worms, sponges, and other simple creatures. Four hundred and fifty million years ago the sea was full of jellyfishes and the first soft-bodied creatures with the beginnings of legs. Another fifty million years afterwards came the squids and sea urchins, and hard on their heels came the first animals which had started to develop the beginnings of a skeleton to keep them firm and stiff.

Three hundred million years back from the present the fishes were the leading forms of life. They were the first creatures to have a proper skeleton inside, and this skeleton was necessary before any animals could manage to creep awkwardly out of the water and live on the dry land. And so, while the tall horse-tails were just starting to grow in the steamy swamps, the land first had animals upon it, and from these creatures all the land animals with backbones have come. The forty-ton *Brontosaurus,* long extinct, the mouse and the monkey, the elephant and panda, the horse and the skunk, all are descended from these first creatures of the land. So too was the *Ichthyosaurus* whose bones had first made me interested in Genesis, but he was a creature which had returned to living in the sea, from which his own ancestors had painfully emerged many millions of years before.

Some creatures gradually managed to take to the air as birds a hundred million years ago, but fifty million years ago others of the land animals returned to their watery home of old to become the

whales, the largest creatures found on the Earth today.

And God blessed them, saying, "Be fruitful and multiply and fill the waters in the seas, and let birds multiply on the earth." And there was evening and there was morning, a fifth day. And God said, "Let the earth bring forth living creatures according to their kinds: cattle and creeping things and beasts of the earth according to their kinds." And it was so. And God made the beasts of the earth according to their kinds and the cattle according to their kinds, and everything that creeps upon the ground according to its kind. And God saw that it was good.

There are more than a half a million different kinds of animals alive on the Earth today, from the myriads of tiny water creatures visible only under a microscope, to the great whales of the Antarctic, and the sparrows of the cities. Many of them exist in vast numbers. Often there are more worms in a single field than there are people in the whole of New York City. The little red-eyed fruit-fly that flits above a pile of apples may produce a family of eight hundred in less than a month, and com-

pared with the sparrows or starlings humans are rare indeed.

The Genesis writer certainly hit upon the great special characteristic of all living things in the phrase 'God blessed them, saying, "Be fruitful and multiply." ' We do not always realize that unless a living thing, whether plant or animal, were able to breed and produce the next generation, then as soon as it reached old age it would become extinct. There would be no young ones to carry on the line.

The new generation in all except the very humblest forms of life is raised from eggs. Usually when we think of eggs we call to mind hens' eggs in a box in the kitchen or a blackbird's eggs in a nest, without realizing that practically every other creature has eggs as well. Actually, we hardly ever have a meal without eating food which is made from eggs of one kind or another. Apart from hens' eggs, most of these eggs are not of animals, but of plants —for every seed is really a plant egg, and seeds form a large proportion of our diet. Peas and beans, oatmeal and corn flakes, bread, rice pudding and the pips in raspberry jam remind us of the tremendous output of eggs by living things. Our most precious fluid, milk, though not made from eggs, is a product which the cow makes in order to nourish her own young in the course of being fruitful and multiplying.

Nor are birds and reptiles the only animals which produce eggs. Flies have eggs, which can often be seen as tiny white objects shaped like sacks of flour, and grouped in bunches on meat or fish which has been exposed too long. The eggs of cabbage white butterflies infest our vegetable gardens, and frogs have eggs which turn into curious little tadpoles. But—and this is what we often fail to realize—cats and mice and cows and elephants all have eggs, with just the minor difference that they hatch and grow inside the body of the mother, so that she gives birth not to an egg which will later break out of a shell as a young creature, but to a young live creature which is already more or less the same shape as herself.

Each new life begins as an egg. And the greatest wonder of the creation of life on the Earth is the astonishing reliability with which every living thing, whether plant or animal, can reproduce itself and bring up generation after generation by this wonderful process which spans the millions of centuries.

8: THE FINAL WONDER

Then God said, "Let us make man in our image, after our likeness; and let them have dominion over the fish of the sea, and over the birds of the air, and over the cattle, and over all the earth, and over every creeping thing that creeps upon the earth." So God created man in his own image, in the image of God he created him; male and female he created them.

This was the climax of the whole creation. At last something quite different was formed upon the Earth. This new creature was Man, who was far above all the other living things which had come before him.

When the Genesis writer spoke of God as saying 'Let us make man in our *image*' he did not mean 'in the same shape.'

An 'image' really means a picture or a reflection, and the Genesis writer saw in human beings a picture or reflection of some of the wonderful nature of

God himself—not in the shape and size of their bodies but in the way in which they can know right from wrong, and love other people. Both of these are things which particularly belong to God's nature. Many people may spend all their lives doing wrong, or hating other people, but this does not mean that they could not be much better 'images' of God if they took the trouble to try.

Humans, like most other animals, are male and female, he and she. But besides this we—as God's 'image'—are able to love in a way that animals can not do, and so we can have all the wonderful excitement and happiness of being father or mother, brother or sister, husband or wife in a family, each helping and loving the others in all sorts of big and little ways, all our lives. Without the great fact that there are two sexes, none of this special happiness would be ours, and the Genesis writer was very wise when he coupled the idea of there being two sexes with the fact that humans were a special reflection of God's own nature.

Man is also like God, 'in the image of God,' because

fishes amphibians · reptiles birds mammals

katimeria

brontosaurus ichthyosaurus barylambda whale

he is always trying to continue God's work of creating, not only in having his own family but in making wonderful things as well. It is only men, not monkeys or bumblebees, who add new and lovely things to the world by writing stories, making fine pieces of music, painting beautiful pictures or building lovely houses and castles and cathedrals, and setting the world ablaze with ideas of freedom and justice for all others, everywhere.

There have been men and women on the Earth for quite a short time. A million years ago there were still no real men, although jellyfish had been flopping in the seas for five hundred times as long. Man is so new that if you could count back in your own family, beyond your father and grandfather, for about three hundred generations, you would find yourself among simple savages without houses, or carts, or knitting, or anything but the simplest tools of stone and wood.

But it is not surprising that Man is so new. His brain and his fingers, his eyes and his memory—these things are so very wonderful and complicated that it took nearly a thousand million years to produce them, one at a time, and little by little, in the creatures from which he is descended.

The brain of a person is the most wonderful thing in the world. It is made of hundreds of millions of separate parts. It can do sums, think up stories, remember friends, learn Latin and French, invent machines, understand books and even try to understand God's purposes, which is what the Genesis writer was trying to do more than two thousand years ago, and what every man and woman, or boy and girl can try to do today. No animals, nor any machine, can do a thousandth part of what we can do with our brains, nor anything so worth while.

Our Genesis writer saw that God meant Man not just to be clever, but to look after the Earth and all its other creatures. This is what he wrote:—

And God blessed them, and God said to them, "Be fruitful and multiply, and fill the earth and subdue it; and have dominion over the fish of the sea and over the birds of the air and over every living thing that moves upon the earth."

The first of the animals to be used by men was certainly the dog, which became his friend six thousand years ago, and although most dogs nowadays are just kept as pets, others are used to do special jobs. Bloodhounds are used for tracking thieves, and the police also use German shepherds for rescuing people from drowning, and for catching bur-

glars. Some dogs are guides to the blind; others round up sheep for the shepherds, or pull sledges for the eskimos. I have even seen a dog go through a train with a collection box, asking for money for children who needed help.

Horses and oxen, sheep and goats, the yak and the camel, pig and cow, ducks and geese and hens, the carrier pigeons flying with important messages, tiny flies in the greenhouse protecting tomatoes from other insects, silkworms spinning their wonderful threads, and spiders making fine strands for instruments used by scientists—these are just a few of the animals which man has put to work for his own use, in return for which he has provided them with food and shelter and safety.

And God said, "Behold, I have given you every plant yielding seed which is upon the face of all the earth, and every tree with seed in its fruit; you shall have them for food. And to every beast of the earth, and to every bird of the air, and to everything that creeps on the earth, everything that has the breath of life, I have given every green plant for food." And it was so.

As we have already seen, all the animals upon the Earth really depend upon the plants, which form the food of most of them. Even fierce animals such as lions, which only eat other animals, need the plants too, because without the plants there would be none of these other creatures for them to eat.

But Man uses the plants more than any other creature does, and by years of careful farming and cross-
ing he has raised splendid varieties of the wheat and
other grains which provide our oatmeal, bread and
cake, and vegetables such as tomatoes and cauli-
flowers, and fine fruits like the Temple orange
and Golden Delicious apple.

And Man has lots of other uses for plants, besides
food. Cotton, linen, sacking, cigarettes, newspapers
and writing paper, baseball bats and the sportsman's
fishing rod are all made from plants. Furniture and
hen-houses, sugar and tea, coffee, chocolate, auto-
mobile tires and ropes—these are only a few of
the things which Man makes from plants which
are alive today.

We can even go back into the past and use the
plants which have been extinct for millions of years.
The fossil plants of the coal seams give us the gas
to cook our meals, and the coke for our heating,
and they also provide bright dyes for our clothes,
sweet scents, and aspirins for headaches; the remains of plants in oil deposits provide gasoline and
oils for automobiles, trucks and aircraft. Our uses
for plants are tremendous.

*And God saw everything that he had made, and
behold, it was very good.*

'Very good.' Yes, very good indeed. Perhaps the
Genesis writer could find no word which would
really express his feeling about the creation. 'Very
good' seems almost too weak an adjective, but

'wonderful' or 'marvellous' would not really have been as suitable. It always seems to me that the great point which he tries to bring out again and again throughout the chapter is not just how wonderful and clever everything is, but that it is *good,* in the fullest sense of the word. Good because it made sense, good because it was useful, good because it reflected God's tremendous power and purpose, but especially because it gave to humans the chance of living as reflections of God himself, and of carrying on his work.

And that surely is the climax of this great story of the creation. The Genesis writer made some brilliant guesses at explaining the structure of the universe and the nature of the sky. Sometimes he was right, we know. At other times he could not make such good guesses as we can do today with all our telescopes and microscopes, and the work of thousands of scientists behind us.

Today we can give a more detailed and truer account of many things which must have puzzled him. But when we look at the story he told us so long ago, we can see that he felt that what is really important about the universe is not the size of the stars, or where the rain comes from, but the fact that it was created by God on purpose, and that we ourselves were made as images or reflections of God's nature.

And if we are images of a creator, then it is up to us to create, and to create good things too. All the things that happened in those distant millions of years were only the beginning. The stars and the

Sun, the Earth and the volcanoes, the water and the early living creatures, all these were the beginning, paving the way for the great time when we ourselves could share in the creation of everything that is good and fine.

We live at the end of the beginning. The world will go on into the future, and what is created upon it in the way of good things and bad things depends no longer upon God alone, but on the way in which each one of us does something to make the creation still more wonderful than it was before, helping to fulfil the purpose of the millions of years which lie behind us.

The writer of that first chapter of Genesis had no doubts about the purpose of everything. It was that everything might be good, very good—the universe, the sky and the seas, the creatures and the flowers, and above all, our own individual lives, as reflections of God's infinite goodness and love.

DESIGNED BY

LOUISE E. JEFFERSON